# Children
# and Trauma

...........................................................

Equipping Parents
and Caregivers

Justin S. Holcomb and
Lindsey A. Holcomb

New
Growth
Press

newgrowthpress.com

New Growth Press, Greensboro, NC 27404
newgrowthpress.com

Cover Design: Tom Temple, tandemcreative.com
Interior Design and Typesetting: Gretchen Logterman

ISBN: 978-1-64507-094-8 (Print)
ISBN: 978-1-64507-095-5 (eBook)

Library of Congress Cataloging-in-Publication Data
Names: Holcomb, Justin S., 1973- author. | Holcomb, Lindsey A., 1981- author.
Title: Children and trauma : equipping parents and caregivers / by Justin S. Holcomb and Lindsey A. Holcomb.
Description: Greensboro, NC : New Growth Press, [2021] | Includes bibliographical references. | Summary: "Justin and Lindsey Holcomb help parents and caregivers recognize the signs of trauma and know how to step into these children's lives and tangibly demonstrate Jesus's love and protect them"-- Provided by publisher.
Identifiers: LCCN 2021008992 (print) | LCCN 2021008993 (ebook) | ISBN 9781645070948 (print) | ISBN 9781645070955 (ebook)
Subjects: LCSH: Parent and child--Religious aspects--Christianity. | Psychic trauma in children--Religious aspects--Christianity. | Caregivers--Religious life.
Classification: LCC BV4529 .H6285 2021 (print) | LCC BV4529 (ebook) | DDC 248.8/45--dc23
LC record available at https://lccn.loc.gov/2021008992
LC ebook record available at https://lccn.loc.gov/2021008993

Printed in India

28 27 26 25 24 23 22 21    1 2 3 4 5

Kayla was five years old when she first suffered sexual abuse by her father. As he tucked her in bed at night, her father would often molest her. Soon after the abuse started, Kayla began wetting the bed on a nightly basis. She had been a generally outgoing, playful, and talkative child, but in the weeks following the abuse, Kayla progressively withdrew from others, spending most of her time sitting quietly off to the side at school. Her appetite shrank and she cried whenever her mother had to leave her—even if it was just for a few minutes.

David was ten when his family lost their house in a fire. He woke up at 2:00 a.m. to the piercing sound of firetruck sirens and his mother and father yelling for David and his older sister, Beth. Normally a thoughtful, quiet boy who did well in school both academically and socially, he suddenly became anxious and irritable. Struggling to pay attention in class and keep up with homework, David began carrying around a backpack full of his most precious possessions, never unpacking it or leaving it out of sight. His anxiety made it difficult for him to fall asleep at night as he stared out the window from his bed, watching for any sign of another fire.

Aiden was fifteen when his mother was diagnosed with cancer. After school, he often helped around the house when his father was working and his mother was too sick from chemo to get out of bed. From preparing dinner to helping his two younger sisters with their homework, Aiden was calm, respectful, and responsible. At school, however, his grades slipped and he began to argue with his teachers. He gradually stopped hanging out with his friends, because their lives seemed so much easier and happier than his. He also stopped attending church and youth group, telling his pastor that he would care about God again when God proved to him that he cared about his mom.

## Ways Children Can Experience Trauma

Kayla, David, and Aiden are just three examples of how trauma leaves a lasting effect on children. There are so many more stories. Understanding a traumatized child starts with understanding what they are going through. Trauma results from events or circumstances that are experienced by a child as physically or emotionally harmful or life-threatening. These experiences have a lasting adverse effect on the child's healthy functioning and mental, physical, social, emotional, and/or spiritual well-being.[1]

Children can experience trauma from a variety of experiences, including but not limited to:

- Natural disasters
- War
- Terrorism
- Community violence
- Vehicle accidents
- Experiencing physical, sexual, or psychological abuse
- Witnessing physical, sexual, or psychological abuse
- Death of a loved one
- Neglect
- Bullying
- Family or intimate partner violence
- Loss, death, or separation from a loved one
- Medical procedures, illnesses, or injuries
- Racial trauma
- Historical trauma
- Migration
- Experiences related to unstable housing or poverty
- Experiences related to being adopted or placed in foster care
- Experiences related to loved one's military service
- Experiences related to identifying as LGBTQ
- Experiences related to disability

The Child Welfare Information Gateway describes trauma as

> an emotional response to an intense event that threatens or causes harm. The harm can be physical or emotional, real or perceived, and it can threaten the child or someone close to him or her. . . . Trauma occurs when a stressful experience (such as being abused, neglected, or bullied) overwhelms the child's natural ability to cope. These events cause a "fight, flight, or freeze" response, resulting in changes in the body—such as faster heart rate and higher blood pressure—as well as changes in how the brain perceives and responds to the world.[2]

Broadly, children can suffer trauma by being exposed to an experience perceived as threatening or harmful and feeling intense fear or being overwhelmed.

## Common Negative Effects of Trauma on Children

It's important to know what negative effects trauma can have on children as a whole. This helps us know how to bring hope and comfort to children as they deal with the fallout of what they have experienced. We want children to know that instead of denying, minimizing, or ignoring what happened to them, God mourns what happened. Through Jesus, God identifies with them and has compassion. God doesn't minimize their pain; he doesn't ignore their hurt. He knows their suffering. He sees, responds, and wants them to know the sorrow and grief he has for their situation.

We want to encourage children to not be silent or deny what happened to them, but to feel and express their emotions, to cry or weep, and to grieve the destruction they have experienced. God has compassion for those who suffer trauma, and at the root of his compassion is the fact that he witnesses their suffering. Psalm 10 reminds us that God sees trouble and grief, and will defend those who have suffered (v. 14).

It's also important to know the effects of trauma so that you can recognize what's happening and understand how certain behaviors, reactions, or difficulties children experience might be a result of their experience. Dealing with the trauma will, in turn, help resolve these issues. Awareness helps create an attitude of compassion and understanding.

## Effects on the Body

There are a number of ways that trauma affects children's bodies. Exposure to a traumatic event or series of chronic traumatic events activates the body's stress response systems that direct the body's attention toward protecting against threats, such as "fight, flight, or freeze" reactions.[3] While these responses can be adaptive and help the individual survive, "prolonged activation of the stress response systems can disrupt the development of brain architecture and other organ systems."[4] These disrupted response systems, which increase levels of stress hormones, impact brain development in children.[5] Childhood trauma can affect the expression of genes and "premature cellular aging," both of which can contribute to health problems into adulthood.[6] Trauma can affect children's immune systems and lead to inflammation in adulthood that is associated with numerous health issues.[7] The type, duration, and severity of trauma impacts which bodily structures and processes are affected and how.

## Effects on Day-to-Day Functioning

Additionally, the impact of trauma on brain development can affect children's day-to-day functioning. The areas of the brain most affected are those involved in stress response, emotional regulation, attention, cognition, executive function, and memory. Childhood trauma, adversity, and toxic stress "are correlated with poor emotional regulation, aggression, hyperactivity, inattention, impulsivity, and dissociation between thought and emotion."[8] These characteristics can affect children's daily lives in numerous ways, including their experiences in school, their relationships, and their engagement in risky behaviors.

Although research indicates associations between child trauma and these behaviors and health problems, it is important to stress that this does not mean all children who experience trauma will experience these outcomes. While this is a serious and necessary topic to cover, it would be incorrect to assume that all children who experience trauma will experience the worst possible outcomes as a result; there is always hope that this will be avoided. A deeper understanding of these risk factors offer hope that healing will come more quickly.

## Spiritual Effects

A child's relationship with God can be profoundly affected by trauma. Children think concretely, not abstractly. They learn about abstract concepts like security, trust, truth, and love from the concrete experiences they have with significant others in their lives. Trauma can disrupt a child's developmental ability to grasp the idea of a loving and trustworthy heavenly Father.

Children (like adults) learn about the unseen, or spiritual, by way of the seen. When a child's concrete experience of the world is marred by trauma, their perception of spiritual realities and their understanding of God—both very abstract concepts—are affected.

Trauma can cause spiritual injuries, including feelings of guilt, anger, grief, despair, fear of death, and a belief that God is unfair.[9] Age also makes a difference, with young children being more spiritually impacted than older children—perhaps because their spirituality is still in development. No matter the age of the child, parents and caregivers can help redefine the labels of love, trust, and truth for children through concrete experiences and interactions.

## Helping Children Recover

What response can parents, caregivers, counselors, and pastors give that will be powerful enough to overcome the above obstacles? If simply speaking or teaching the truth is not sufficient, then what else is required?

Because of the spiritual impact of trauma, parents, caregivers, counselors, or pastors will need to learn thoughtful approaches that will be powerful enough to help children overcome the hurt that trauma has brought into their lives.

While trauma can have spiritual effects, a child's faith can be a source of resiliency and may help a traumatized child cope physically and emotionally with their trauma. Rather than minimize grief, Jesus experiences it and offers profound comfort. He leads the way in mourning—giving us a model of how to go to God with our grief. But he doesn't just show us how to cry out to God. He mourns with us. You can remind children that Jesus wept when he was at Lazarus's grave. Even though he was going to raise him from the dead, he cried because of the sorrow of his friends (John 11:35).

But because of Jesus, mourning is not the final word—resurrection is. The knowledge of his resurrection is our sure hope in the middle of deep sorrow. Our grief now is in the context of a future hope. Jesus encourages his followers, "Let not your hearts be troubled. Believe in God; believe also in me. In my Father's house are many rooms. If it were not so, would I have told you that I go to prepare a place for you? And if I go and prepare a place for you, I will come again and will take you to myself, that where I am you may be also" (John 14:1–3).

The hope of the new creation frames, but does not erase, our present mourning. Revelation 21:3–4 speaks directly to this: "Behold, the dwelling place of God is with man. He will dwell with them, and they will be his people, and God himself will be with them as their God. He will wipe away every tear from their eyes, and death shall be no more, neither shall there be mourning, nor crying, nor pain anymore, for the former things have passed away."

Knowing that God sees, cares for, and understands their suffering will help traumatized children move forward in their healing. Reminding them that one day all pain and suffering will cease can help turn their minds away from any anxieties they may have about future trauma and toward promised future peace and joy.

## Hope for Healing and Growth

Most of the studies on child trauma focus on the negative effects, but there is encouraging research exploring how children grow and experience positive change after traumatic experiences. Posttraumatic growth is defined as "positive change experienced as a result of the struggle with trauma" and tends to occur in the following areas: "a greater sense of one's personal strength; a different perspective on one's relationships; a changed philosophy of life, such as greater appreciation for life and its new possibilities; and spiritual growth."[10]

For a believer, posttraumatic growth can be seen in a few ways. First, God has created us in such a way that we can be resilient in painful and even traumatic situations. Second, growth can happen as we step into a deepened understanding of who God is and what his disposition is toward our suffering. A stronger sense of our identity and worth in Christ, and the ability to go to him in every season of life, allows the peace of Christ to fill the hearts of even the youngest trauma survivors.

While trauma can deeply affect a child's core beliefs about themselves, others, the world, God, and the expected course of life, it is equally true that growth can occur "as one comes to grips with his or her new reality and works to understand what has happened and its implications for life going forward."[11] Many children do experience posttraumatic growth after traumatic events, and there is evidence of greater posttraumatic growth among religious youth.[12] If you are in the middle of walking through trauma with your child, our hope is that as you grieve with them you will find peace and hope not only in statistics but in God's power to heal and restore what's been harmed.

Mourn. Grieve. Cry. God is grieved by and angry at what happened to your child (see Psalms 9–10, 37–40). He is even more grieved and angry than you are, so you are invited to participate with God in his grief and anger. That is why your cry does not need to be one of despair but can be one of hope and faith. While the cross shows us that God understands pain and does not judge you or your child for your feelings of grief, the resurrection shows that God is active in restoring peace, that he conquered sin, and that he is actively reversing its effects.

## Manifestations of Trauma

Because trauma involves feeling threatened and overwhelmed and also causes physical changes in the body, it is understandable that children typically exhibit strong or different emotions and behaviors following traumatic experiences. Reactions can include fear, anger, avoidance, withdrawal, or aggression.[13]

Trauma can manifest in a variety of different ways in children. Some children react immediately following traumatic events, whereas others may not show signs of distress until weeks later. The intensity and duration of reactions also vary considerably in children, with some recovering quite quickly after a traumatic event and others experiencing long-term effects.[14]

## Young Children

Following a traumatic event, children in the earliest few years of life often experience continuing and pervasive fear, as they may not be able to discern as well when the threat has ended.[15] This may manifest as increased crying, nightmares, or clinginess to parents or caregivers and struggling to be away from them such as at preschool. Young children may seem to regress developmentally or exhibit behaviors they previously outgrew, such as sucking their thumb or wetting the bed.[16] They may also exhibit changes in sleeping or eating behaviors. Some may lose interest in playing with their toys or interacting with people. Others may repeatedly focus on or recreate elements of the traumatic event when they play.[17]

## Elementary School-Aged Children

Children in this age group may become increasingly anxious and worried about the safety of themselves and others following a traumatic event.[18] They may deal with feelings of shame or guilt related to the experience. Many children have difficulty paying attention, which can lead to challenges in school. Some may develop aches and pains with no clearly identifiable medical cause, or experience sleep disturbances such as nightmares or difficulty falling asleep.[19] Others may startle easily or engage in aggressive behavior.

## Adolescents

Due to the many changes children already experience in this developmental stage, adolescents may struggle with healthy coping and relationships following a traumatic event.[20] To avoid feeling weak, vulnerable, or different than their peers, some may try to pretend like they are okay while others may withdraw.[21] Adolescents may experience intense feelings such as shame, depression, or desires for revenge following a traumatic event.[22] Additionally, some in this developmental stage may become increasingly argumentative or engage in self-harm or in risky behaviors such as alcohol or drug use.[23]

## God's Care for Children

As we explore the ways children suffer from trauma, it is critical that we understand God's care for them, so that we can help teach and manifest the heavenly Father's love and concern toward the hurting young people in our lives.

Scripture has an incredibly high view of children. Jesus praised the humility and simple faith of little ones, and exhorted adult believers to imitate their humble and straightforward approach to God (Matthew 18:1–4). He also indicated that children can perceive spiritual matters that the "wise and understanding" cannot (Matthew 11:25). Likewise, in Psalm 8:2, King David highlights the glory God receives when little children praise him.

Part of God's law, given at Mount Sinai, was that no one should "mistreat any widow or fatherless child" (Exodus 22:22). Indeed, God is one who "executes justice for the fatherless" (Deuteronomy 10:18) and curses anyone who perverts the justice due to orphans (Deuteronomy 27:19). The Lord says that no one should do wrong or be violent toward innocent children and orphans (Jeremiah 22:3). Not only does God want his people to love and care for children, but he calls them to do everything in their power to stop those who try to hurt, abuse, or oppress them: "learn to do good; seek justice, correct oppression; bring justice to the fatherless, plead the widow's cause" (Isaiah 1:17). Children are a gift from God (Psalm 127:3) and a blessing; they are to be loved and protected.

The tenderness and care Jesus showed for children during his earthly ministry is an expression of God's heart toward the small, the weak, and the vulnerable seen through-out the Old Testament. In fact, Jesus often included them in his teaching, to the surprise of his disciples. In addition to his instruction about humility, he emphasized to the disci-ples that part of their duty was to receive little children, and insisted that it would be better for the person who causes a child to sin to be drowned in the sea than to continue living (Matthew 18:5–6; Luke 17:2). Later in the Matthew passage, Jesus says that children have a special place in God's heart: "See that you do not despise one of these little ones. For I tell you that in heaven their angels always see the face of my Father who is in heaven" (Matthew 18:10).

When people were bringing children to Jesus so that he would pray for them, the disciples rebuked these people, thinking that Jesus had better things to do (Matthew 19:13). To their surprise, Jesus insisted, "Let the little chil-dren come to me and do not hinder them, for to such belongs the kingdom of heaven" (Matthew 19:14).

Part of Jesus's ministry on earth involved healing chil-dren. In Mark 5:39, Jesus came into the house of a ruler of the synagogue, whose daughter had just died. Jesus said that she was not dead but only sleeping. After they laughed at him, Jesus said to the child, "Little girl, I say to you, arise" (Mark 5:41). Mark recounts what happened next: "And immediately the girl got up and began walking (for she was twelve years of age), and they were immediately overcome with amazement" (Mark 5:42). Similarly, in Mark 9, Jesus encounters a young boy who had been having demonic attacks. Jesus commanded the unclean spirit to come out of him (Mark 9:25), and the boy fell down as if he were dead. Jesus took him by the hand and he was healed (Mark 9:27). Jesus, who calls himself "the resurrection and the life" (John 11:25), brings life and healing to children.

## Helping Children Who Have Experienced Trauma

Jesus wants his followers to honor, protect, and care for those among them who are small and vulnerable, especially children. Jesus referred to children as messengers from God and made it clear that our treatment of children speaks volumes about what we really believe about God (Mark 9:36–37).

In the Bible, God is One who stands with the vulnerable and powerless and speaks judgment against those who choose to use their power in ways that harm others. The oppressor unjustly uses force and deceit to take from the vulnerable. They think that no one cares and that no one will interfere with their plans. But God's interest in the abuse of power is not passive. He is not at all resigned to injustice in a fallen world. The misuse of power to harm the vulnerable strikes against God's holiness. Many passages in the Bible speak out against violence and about God's attitude toward those who repeatedly use it (Psalm 11:5; 37:9; Zephaniah 1:9; Malachi 2:6).

God's wrath is a source of positive hope for the victims of trauma. They need to know that God loves them and will destroy the evil that has harmed them. God is the refuge of his people and shows steadfast love by destroying those who "strike terror" (Psalm 10:18). The wrath of God in the Bible is often presented not as something to fear, but as something on which to set your hope, as the consolation, refuge, and deliverance of God's suffering people (Mark 9:43–49; Romans 12:17–21; Colossians 3:6; Hebrews 10:26–31; 2 Peter 3:10–12; Revelation 11:18; 15:1–8; 16:1–21).

However, as we lean into God's justice and help those in our care, we also remember that God's justice often includes going to the proper authorities to report such abuses. In cases of abuse, we should use the authorities to help the vulnerable, weak, and abused among us. Failure to do so allows perpetrators to continue their cycle of abuse.

As we react with shock and horror to the many ways in which children suffer trauma, we should be driven to step into these children's lives, tangibly demonstrate Jesus's love, and protect them. God's deep love and concern for children should spur us to imitate his tender care for them and to offer them hope and a sense of safety.

The compassionate and helpful response of parents or caregivers can help children who have experienced trauma to access spiritual, emotional, and physical healing. "How a community responds to individual trauma sets the foundation for the impact of the traumatic event, experience, and effect. Communities that provide a context of understanding and self-determination may facilitate the healing and recovery process for the individual. Alternatively, communities that avoid, overlook, or misunderstand the impact of trauma may often be re-traumatizing and interfere with the healing process. Individuals can be re-traumatized by the very people whose intent is to be helpful."[24] How amazing it would be if the youngest victims could find healing and hope in their church community!

## Positive and Healing Behaviors

There are a number of ways that a parent or caregiver's helpful, compassionate response encourages a child's healing process. First, trauma survivors benefit from feeling safe. One of five core principles recommended for effective interventions after disasters and violence is to "promote a sense of safety."[25]

Second, sensitive, responsive care from parents and caregivers helps young children's stress response systems. This kind of engaged and nurturing care has been associated with lower stress hormones, resilience, and better adjustment in children.[26]

In addition to this, research has shown that parental responses of "positive reframing, emotional expression, and acceptance were associated with lower distress levels."[27]

## Negative and Harmful Behaviors

In addition to these positive parenting behaviors, there are also some negative behaviors to avoid as you respond and seek to help a hurting child.

First, it is important to avoid overprotective parenting, as this has been known to encourage posttraumatic stress symptoms in children.[28] Overprotective parenting is guarding behavior that is considered excessive when considering the child's developmental stage and actual risk in their setting. This happens when a parent's level of protection exceeds the much lower level of actual risk. Although helping ensure the safety of children is vital after traumatic experiences, it is possible that excessive protection may diminish children's sense of autonomy and self-efficacy, and thus potentially hinder their healing.

Secondly, parents should be conscious of how they speak about their children in front of them. Telling them they're permanently changed or vulnerable will only negatively impact them and ingrain the idea that their trauma is insurmountable. It can exacerbate their distress and influence how they speak about themselves, creating an unhealthy identity while leading to hopelessness and poor self-esteem. Help children separate their trauma from their worth as people made in God's image. Though it plays a sad part in their story, it does not define them.

## Additional Recommendations

While the specific responses children need will vary, there is a wealth of general advice to help parents and caregivers respond well and help children heal. The following recommendations are geared toward situations where the traumatic event has ended and children are in a reasonably safe environment.[29]

- Provide children with safety and reassure them that they are safe. Give them examples of what you have done to help protect them at home or school.[30] This might include walking them to their classroom every day, remaining within earshot whenever you're at home, watching them play outside so they're not alone, and waiting for them at the entrance of the school or the bus stop to pick them up.
- Help children feel connected and loved. Tell and show them you love them and will try your best to take care of them.[31] This includes being emotionally and physically available (hugs, time together as a family, etc.).[32] Reassure children it is normal to have a lot of different or strong feelings after a traumatic event.
- Let children know that what happened was not their fault, and be an attentive and nonjudgmental

listener. Allow children to process their experience and express their feelings. This could mean helping children find words or encouraging opportunities for them to express themselves through talking, writing, playing, music, or other activities. Do not be dismissive of their feelings or encourage children to simply get over them.[33]

- Pray with children.
- Provide professional care for children when needed. This includes, therapists, CPS workers, mental health professionals, victim-witness advocates, school guidance counselors, or social workers.
- Provide professional investigators when appropriate. This includes informing the authorities when there is known or suspected child abuse.
- When children are upset or exhibiting strong emotions, try to respond calmly rather than react in anger. Remain supportive, speak in a steady and reassuring voice, and acknowledge their feelings.[34] Try not to take children's behaviors personally. Remember that children may be engaging in responses that feel automatic to them or that they feel powerless to control, and the behaviors may have protected themselves or others during the traumatic event(s).[35]
- Return to usual routines, when possible and still helpful. These might include mealtimes, school, weekend activities, or bedtime routines. Try to be consistent, such as picking children up on time and letting them know in advance about any changes.[36]
- Give children some control in daily activities, appropriate to their age and developmental stage. Allow them to make some choices about clothes, meals, etc.[37]

- Encourage children about their security in Christ. If they have faith in Christ, their identity is secure and robust. God conveys value on his children by reminding them that they have been adopted into his family. This identity goes deeper than any of their wounds. This truth brings great relief, because they are not doomed to live as victims of trauma. It doesn't eliminate their wounds nor silence their cries for deliverance or healing, but it does mean those wounds are not the final word on who they are.

- Engage the feeling of anger. God's anger against sin and its effects is justified. That God is angry tells us something important: "Anger can be utterly right, good, appropriate, beautiful, the only fair response to something evil, and the loving response on behalf of evil's victims."[38] God's people can also express godly anger: "Be angry and do not sin" (Ephesians 4:26). Telling children that God is angry when they experience trauma can be encouraging.

- Offer hope. Rather than being simply a desire for a particular guaranteed outcome, hope is characterized by certainty in the Bible. Hope is sure because God is behind the promise, and he has provided faithfully in the past to his people. The hope you need right now borrows from God's faithfulness in the past and anticipation of it in the future. The basis you have for hope is the resurrection of Jesus from the dead.

## Conclusion

As followers of Christ, we are called to care for the weak, vulnerable, and hurting. Children who experience trauma are, sadly, a prime example of this. They are a sobering reminder of the reality that things in the world are not as they should be. Too often children have been passed off as a nuisance and a burden, some*thing* to be "seen and not heard." But the Bible shows us that a child is some*one* made in the image of God and deserving of our care and attention.

Grace, hope, and healing are available because Jesus went through the valley of the shadow of death and rose from death. The gospel engages our life with all its pain, shame, rejection, lostness, sin, and death. So now, to your pain, God says, "You will be healed." To any shame, God says, "You can now come to God in confidence." To any rejection, God says, "You are accepted!" To any lostness, God says, "You are found and I won't ever let you go."

As you seek to care for the children in your midst who are dealing with trauma, or to help others care for these children, I would encourage you to remember that you are not alone and God will have the final say. One day, he will put all things right. Until then, it is our privilege and calling to provide safety, comfort, and hope for those afflicted, and to walk patiently through this process with them as individuals made and beloved by the God who created the universe and holds it in his hands.

> Almighty God, who created us in your image: Grant us grace fearlessly to contend against evil and to make no peace with oppression; and, that we may reverently use our freedom, help us to employ it in the maintenance of justice in our communities and among the nations, to the glory of your holy Name; through Jesus Christ our Lord, who lives and reigns with you and the Holy Spirit, one God, now and for ever. *Amen.*
>
> *Book of Common Prayer*

# Endnotes

1. Substance Abuse and Mental Health Services Administration, Trauma and Justice Strategic Initiative, *SAMHSA's Concept of Trauma and Guidance for a Trauma-Informed Approach* (Washington, DC: U.S. Department of Health and Human Services, 2014), 7, https://store.samhsa.gov/system/files/sma14-4884.pdf.

2. Child Welfare Information Gateway, "Parenting a Child Who Has Experienced Trauma," U.S. Department of Health and Human Services, Children's Bureau (2014), 2, https://www.child-welfare.gov/pubPDFs/child-trauma.pdf.

3. Michael D. De Bellis and Abigail Zisk, "The Biological Effects of Childhood Trauma," *Child and Adolescent Psychiatric Clinics* 23:2 (2014), 185–222.

4. American Academy of Pediatrics, "Adverse Childhood Experiences and the Lifelong Consequences of Trauma" (2014), 2, https://www.aap.org/en-us/Documents/ttb_aces_consequences.pdf.

5. Michael D. De Bellis, et al., "The Lifelong Effects of Early Childhood Adversity and Toxic Stress," *Pediatrics* 129:1 (2012), e232–46.

6. David Baumeister, et al., "Childhood Trauma and Adulthood Inflammation: A Meta-Analysis of Peripheral C-Reactive Protein, Interleukin-6 and Tumour Necrosis Factor-α," *Molecular Psychiatry* 21:5 (2016), 642–649; Benoit Labonté, et al., "Genome-Wide Epigenetic Regulation by Early-Life Trauma," *Archives of General Psychiatry* 69:7 (2012), 722–731; Michael D. De Bellis, et al., "Exposure to Violence during Childhood Is Associated with Telomere Erosion from 5 to 10 Years of Age: A Longitudinal Study," *Molecular Psychiatry* 18:5 (2013), 576–81.

7. Baumeister, "Childhood Trauma and Adulthood Inflammation."

8. Moira A. Szilagyi, David S. Rosen, David Rubin, and Sarah Zlotnik, "Health Care Issues for Children and Adolescents in Foster Care and Kinship Care," *Pediatrics*, 136:4 (2015), e1144–45.

9. Ronald Lawson, et al., "The Long Term Impact of Child Abuse on Religious Behavior and Spirituality in Men," *Child Abuse and Neglect* 22 (1998), 369.

10. Ryan P. Kilmer, et al., "Posttraumatic Growth in Children and Youth: Clinical Implications of an Emerging Research Literature," *American Journal of Orthopsychiatry* 84:5 (2014), 506–18.

11. Kilmer, et al., "Posttraumatic Growth in Children and Youth," 507.

12. David A. Meyerson, Kathryn E. Grant, Jocelyn Smith Carter, and Ryan P. Kilmer, "Posttraumatic Growth among Children and Adolescents: A Systematic Review," *Clinical Psychology Review* 31:6 (2011), 949–64; Kilmer, et al., "Posttraumatic Growth in Children and Youth."

13. International Society for Traumatic Stress Studies, "Children and Trauma" (2016). https://istss.org/ISTSS_Main/media/Documents/ISTSS_ChildrenandTrauma_English_FNL.pdf.

14. Child Welfare Information Gateway, "Parenting a Child Who Has Experienced Trauma."

15. The National Child Traumatic Stress Network, "Age-Related Reactions to a Traumatic Event" (2010), 1, https://www.nctsn.org/sites/default/files/resources//age_related_reactions_to_traumatic_events.pdf.

16. Substance Abuse and Mental Health Services Administration, "Tips for Talking with and Helping Children and Youth Cope after a Disaster or Traumatic Event: A Guide for Parents, Caregivers, and Teachers" (2013), https://store.samhsa.gov/system/files/sma12-4732.pdf.

17. National Child Traumatic Stress Network, "Age-Related Reactions to a Traumatic Event."

18. National Child Traumatic Stress Network, "Age-Related Reactions to a Traumatic Event."

19. National Child Traumatic Stress Network, "Age-Related Reactions to a Traumatic Event"; International Society for Traumatic Stress Studies, "Children and Trauma."

20. Substance Abuse and Mental Health Services Administration, "Tips for Talking."

21. Substance Abuse and Mental Health Services Administration, "Tips for Talking"; National Child Traumatic Stress Network, "Age-Related Reactions to a Traumatic Event."

22. National Child Traumatic Stress Network, "Age-Related Reactions to a Traumatic Event"; International Society for Traumatic Stress Studies, "Children and Trauma".

23. Substance Abuse and Mental Health Services Administration, "Tips for Talking"; National Child Traumatic Stress Network, "Age-Related Reactions to a Traumatic Event."

24. Substance Abuse and Mental Health Services Administration, Trauma and Justice Strategic Initiative, *SAMHSA's Concept of Trauma,* 17.

25. Stevan E. Hobfoll, et al., "Five Essential Elements of Immediate and Mid-Term Mass Trauma Intervention: Empirical Evidence," *Psychiatry: Interpersonal and Biological Processes* 70:4 (2007), 285–86.

26. Megan R. Gunnar and Carol L. Cheatham, "Brain and Behavior Interface: Stress and the Developing Brain," *Infant Mental Health Journal* 24:3 (2003), 195–211; Szilagyi, Rosen, Rubin, and Zlotnik, "Health Care Issues for Children and Adolescents in Foster Care and Kinship Care"; Kristin Valentino, Steven Berkowitz, and Carla Smith Stover, "Parenting Behaviors and Posttraumatic Symptoms in Relation to Children's Symptomatology Following a Traumatic Event," *Journal of Traumatic Stress* 23:3 (2010), 403–7.

27. Virginia Gil-Rivas, et al., "Parental Response and Adolescent Adjustment to the September 11, 2001 Terrorist Attacks," *Journal of Traumatic Stress* 20:6 (2007), 1067.

28. Victoria Williamson, et al., "The Role of Parenting Behaviors in Childhood Post-Traumatic Stress Disorder: A Meta-Analytic Review," *Clinical Psychology Review* 53 (2017), 1–13; Anna Bokszczanin, "Parental Support, Family Conflict, and Overprotectiveness: Predicting PTSD Symptom Levels of Adolescents 28 Months after a Natural Disaster," *Anxiety, Stress, & Coping* 21:4 (2008), 325–35.

29. For more detailed practical advice and recommendations, please see the following National Child Traumatic Stress Network webpage: https://www.nctsn.org/resources/all-nctsn-resources. Resources can be narrowed down by specific trauma type and by audience (such as "Families and Caregivers").

30. The National Child Traumatic Stress Network, "Understanding Child Traumatic Stress: A Guide for Parents" (2008), https://www.nctsn.org/sites/default/files/resources//understanding_child_traumatic_stress_guide_for_parents.pdf; International Society for Traumatic Stress Studies.

31. National Institute of Mental Health, "Helping Children and Adolescents Cope with Disasters and Other Traumatic Events: What Parents, Rescue Workers, and the Community Can Do" (n.d). https://www.nimh.nih.gov/health/publications/helping-children-and-adolescents-cope-with-disasters-and-other-traumatic-events/19-mh-8066-helpingchildrenwithdisasters-508_158447.pdf.

32. Child Welfare Information Gateway, "Parenting a Child Who Has Experienced Trauma."

33. Child Welfare Information Gateway, "Parenting a Child Who Has Experienced Trauma."

34. Child Welfare Information Gateway, "Parenting a Child Who Has Experienced Trauma."

35. Child Welfare Information Gateway, "Parenting a Child Who Has Experienced Trauma."

36. Child Welfare Information Gateway, "Parenting a Child Who Has Experienced Trauma"; International Society for Traumatic Stress Studies, "Children and Trauma" (2016); National Institute of Mental Health, "Helping Children and Adolescents Cope"; National Child Traumatic Stress Network, "Understanding Child Traumatic Stress."

37. Child Welfare Information Gateway, "Parenting a Child Who Has Experienced Trauma"; International Society for Traumatic Stress Studies, "Children and Trauma"; National Institute of Mental Health, "Helping Children and Adolescents Cope."

38. David Powlison, "Anger Part 1: Understanding Anger," *The Journal of Biblical Counseling* 14:1 (1995), 40.